MOON'S QUEST

Enlightenment Through Yoga Sutras of Patanjali

Prabha Srinivasan

Balboa Press books may be ordered through booksellers or by contacting:

Balboa Press
A Division of Hay House
1663 Liberty Drive
Bloomington, IN 47403
www.balboapress.com.au
1 (877) 407-4847

ISBN: 978-1-5043-1593-7 (sc)
ISBN: 978-1-5043-1594-4 (e)

Print information available on the last page.

Balboa Press rev. date: 12/05/2018

CONTENTS

DEDICATION

This book is devoted to all aspirants of knowledge, for the courage to step beyond and explore the unknown.

<u>Special mentions</u>

I would like to make few special mentions of thanks,

1. To all students of Yoga Philosophy study group at Hridhaya Centre, for enabling me to write this book.
2. To my mother, Usha, for always believing in me and supporting me in all my endeavours whatever they happen to be.
3. To my father, Srinivasan, for being the hidden catalyst behind all my achievements in life.
4. To my son, Rishadh, for propelling my spiritual journey through his appearance and presence in my life.

INTRODUCTION

While Yoga is commonly known for various poses and relaxation benefits, the purpose of Yoga is mostly unknown and hardly taught in today's world. This book aims at giving you a deep understanding of the philosophy of Yoga buried in the Yoga Sutras of Patanjali. Yoga has existed ever since man has, however a sage named Patanjali consolidated the practice of Yoga into what is known as the Yoga Sutras consisting of 4 chapters with roughly 50 aphorisms each.

The purpose of this book is to present to you, various techniques and stages of self-realisation described in the Yoga Sutras. All interpretations of the Yoga Sutras provided in this book is drawn from various sources including interpretations of various teachers and most importantly my own lived experience of accessing the inner wisdom.

In 2016, I published my first book, Guidance in Your Handbag, which contains a collection of 100 insights that came to me through meditation. While these insights were very relevant for me and those who purchased my books, it was a mystery to me as to how I was accessing these insights. My intuition seemed to be nudging me towards Yoga to help me solve this mystery. So, I went to India and undertook Yoga teacher training with a quest to understand the process behind what I unknowingly achieved through meditation. During the Yoga teacher training I was introduced to Yoga Sutras of Patanjali and in reading the Sutras, I felt a compelling pull. Upon further research and reflecting on the meaning of the sutra, I found answers to my burning questions. That experience inspired me to publish this book.

Yoga Sutras serve as guide book for all aspirants of self-realisation. It is my aim that this book will enable your self-realisation journey by bringing to you the wisdom hidden in the Yoga Sutras.

Please bear in mind that all interpretations provided in this book are my perspective of the Yoga Sutras and not the ultimate perspective. I understand some of my interpretations may contradict other popular interpretations and I request you to take all recommendations with a pinch of salt and apply your own discernment.

Some guidelines to understand and use this book:

1. As Swami Rama says, Yoga Sutra is a curriculum designed for Yoga teachers to facilitate the journey for their students. Although it is possible, it is not recommended for Yoga students to use the Yoga Sutra in attempt to teach themselves. The reason for this being that, like all other things in life, enlightenment too is a journey from the known to the unknown and it can be confusing, confronting and challenging. With the help of a teacher who can lead through lived experience of their own journey and in the company of other aspirants, the process can be less daunting and more enjoyable.

2. Yoga Sutra text does not sub divide the chapters into lessons however, I have done so to help students assimilate the enormous chapters in smaller chunks. Thus, the grouping of lessons and the topics chosen for each lesson, is my personal addition.

3. The right-hand side pages of this book have been dedicated for interpretations of the sutra and the left-hand side pages have been dedicated to present some additional relevant explanation, quotes, poems that are not part of the Yoga Sutra.

4. All quotes and poems presented in italics are my personal additions, to enhance your understanding.

5. For background information, various other philosophical texts have been referred to such as Sankhya Sutra and various Upanishads. All such references made are included on the left-hand side of this book and declared appropriately.

6. Wherever necessary I have inserted extra words in parenthesis, amongst translated words from the Sutra. I have done so to enable full understanding of the cryptic sentences Patanjali uses.

Move into a space where nothing else exists but that.

CHAPTER 1: ABSORPTION (SAMADHI)

LESSON 1: PURPOSE OF YOGA

Now begins the study and practise of Yoga. {1.1}

Yoga is mastery over the tendencies of one's mind. {1.2}

Then one's perception of self, rests in their true nature. {1.3}

At other times, one identifies with their false self. {1.4}

LESSON 2: TENDENCIES OF THE MIND

The mind has 5 main tendencies all of which can be harmful or harmless. {1.5}

The five tendencies of mind are as follows. {1.6}

1. Aligned Conception
2. Distorted Conception
3. Imagination
4. Sleep
5. Memory

Aligned conception (understanding, cognition) can be gained through 3 sources namely, (a) direct perception, (b) inference, (c) passed on from realised souls (testimony) {1.7}

Distorted conception is based on illusionary perception far from the true nature of that which is being perceived. {1.8}

Imagination is based on verbal knowledge for which there is no real existence. {1.9}

Sleep is based on absence of cognition. {1.10}

Memory is the retained impression created by experience. {1.11}

* Sankhya Sutra describes 'guna' as the 3 basic qualities that nature is made of. (See supporting text for lesson 13 for more on Sankhya philosophy) In the context of this lesson, they can be interpreted as *sattva* –fairness, *rajas* - drive, *tamas* - immorality. When one attains a state beyond these three, there is complete acceptance and peace.

Like the two lines of a train track, practise and non-attachment ought to be carried out simultaneously for a long period of time, to overcome the tendencies of one's mind.

LESSON 3: OVERCOMING 5 TENDENCIES OF MIND

The state of yoga can be achieved by following practise and non-attachment simultaneously. {1.12}

The practise mentioned above denotes striving towards steady tranquillity of mind. {1.13}

That practise, when done over a long period of time, without breaks, maintaining a cheerful attitude and perseverance, brings firm grounding (of tranquillity). {1.14}

By freeing oneself from craving for matters seen/heard/understood (through scriptures or tradition), one arrives at the level of consciousness called non-attachment. (In other words, recognising and letting go of tendencies mentioned in 1.7b and 1.7c) {1.15}

Attaining knowledge of the supreme self, one gains freedom from 'guna*. {1.16}

LESSON 4: LEVELS OF COGNITIVE ABSORPTION

Initial levels are experienced in the following order {1.17}

1. new thoughts of peaceful nature
2. new inferences
3. blissfulness and
4. an expanding sense of 'I'ness.

Through the practise of letting go, one reaches the subsequent level, where all arising thoughts, notions, memories can be set aside, allowing the mind to be blank. {1.18}

One can interpret the word 'Supreme' used in this book, to denote the Sanskrit word 'Ishvara' as one's own higher self, the soul, an enlightened being or god.

The Supreme

I am the one who never sleeps.

I am the one who knows it all.

Forever creating and orchestrating

I am the one with a grand plan -

to watch what emerges

out of the flow, of all things

living, been and gone.

If I say it is, then so be it.

If I say it isn't, then so be it too.

Without me, you would not be.

The body and thoughts,

it just ain't me!

LESSON 5: REACHING COGNITIVE ABSORPTION

Some bring it into human life as credit during their incarnation. {1.19}

Others can access this wisdom, by adopting conviction, zeal and intentful remembrance. {1.20}

When one is keen and vigorous, this attainment comes quickly. {1.21}

Time taken also varies depending on the intensity of practise undertaken namely, mild, medium and strong. {1.22}

LESSON 6: SIGNIFICANCE OF OM

It (state of yoga/ oneness/ enlightenment) can also be achieved by surrendering to the Supreme. {1.23}

That Supreme is beyond suffering, action, consequences and desires. {1.24}

There (in the Supreme) lies the seed of all knowledge and limitlessness. {1.25}

That (Supreme) is also the prototype, the guide and is beyond time. {1.26}

That (Supreme) is denoted by the word OM. {1.27}

By chanting and meditating on that word, one can embody its characteristics (mentioned in 1.24, 1.25 & 1.26). {1.28}

Through this practise (mentioned in 1.27) all obstacles vanish and the true self shines through. {1.29}

The oneness principle is the philosophy that we are all one being experiencing life through different bodies and minds. When you face an obstacle that takes you away from your daily 'practise' contemplate on the oneness principle. If we are all one, who is to blame when things aren't going well? If we are one, what do we not have access to including enlightenment?

<u>The Oneness Principle</u>

The preacher is you,

the preached is you.

The criminal is you,

the saviour is you.

The giver is you,

the receiver is you.

When all there is, is you

why condemn?

Judge not, curse not,

offend not, praise not.

Accept, appreciate & adore

the good and the bad.,

for it is all one and the same.

LESSON 7: OBSTACLES

Those obstacles are disturbances in the mind namely, disease, dullness, doubt, materialistic obsession, idleness, craving, false perception, instability, inconsistency. {1.30}

Accompaniments for these obstacles are pain, depression, restlessness in the body and irregular breathing. {1.31}

These obstacles and accompaniments can be overcome by embodying the oneness principle. {1.32}

LESSON 8: BREAKING THROUGH OBSTACLES

The mind can be stabilised by cultivating the following attitudes, {1.33}

1. Friendliness with (those who are) happy
2. Compassion for (those who are) suffering
3. Cheerfulness towards (those who are) blessed
4. Indifference towards the vice

The same (mental stability) can be achieved also by practising breathing techniques (see Lesson 21) . {1.34}

Or by meditating on thoughts, objects, memories that bring about tranquillity. {1.35}

Or by concentrating on pain free luminous state. {1.36}

Or by detaching the mind from that which is causing suffering. {1.37}

Or by bringing oneself to a dreamlike state where supreme knowledge can emerge. {1.38}

Or by meditating on that which one is yearning for. {1.39}

Below is an illustration of the sequence of **<u>Encounter with True Self</u>** as listed in Chapter 1 of Yoga Sutra.

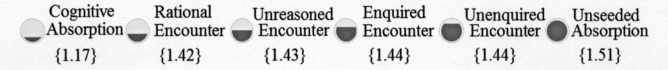

Cognitive Absorption {1.17}   Rational Encounter {1.42}   Unreasoned Encounter {1.43}   Enquired Encounter {1.44}   Unenquired Encounter {1.44}   Unseeded Absorption {1.51}

<u>Unseeded Absorption</u>

I do not exist

the way you see me.

I is a mirage

that just appears to be.

Yet in the projection of your mind

I take form, grim or glee.

Look deeply and you will see,

I am everywhere and yet nowhere,

now, here, if you be.

LESSON 9: ENLIGHTENED STATE

Extending from the finest (atom) to the largest (cosmos), everything comes under one's will. {1.40}

Resulting from minimised mental fluctuations, one becomes a true reflector (a flawless mirror that reflects as is) enabling the perceiver, the act of perceiving and the perceived, to merge. {1.41}

Here one arrives at a stage of *rational* encounter (with All There Is), where testimony and imagination continue to exist in one's awareness. {1.42}

Then comes *unreasoned* encounter, where the memory is purified (uncoloured), the form is nullified (unidentified) and pure understanding shines through. {1.43}

Following on, comes enquired encounter and *un-enquired* encounter where subtle matters are explained to the self. {1.44}

This understanding of subtle matters lead all the way back to source. {1.45}

All the above-mentioned states are seeded* absorption (with All There Is). {1.46}

The state experienced at un-enquired encounter is purity of the soul. {1.47}

Here comes knowledge filled with truth. {1.48}

The understanding thus arrived, is different from testimony and inference (see sutra 1.7). {1.49}

The mental impressions produced at this stage stops further accumulation of unhelpful mental impressions. {1.50}

When this (helpful mental impressions) too fades away, one arrives at unseeded absorption. {1.51}

*To include anything in your life, simply develop
awareness of the part of you that is already one with it.*

---

* To understand the attitude of endurance ('tapa' in Sanskrit) the following example can be considered. Gold is subjected to a process of heating that helps remove impurities and extract the purest gold, which is then made it into various ornaments. In a similar manner, human beings go through various experiences in life that helps them let go of distorted conception (discussed in Lesson 2) and arrive at aligned conception, so they can know themselves.

CHAPTER 2: PRACTISE (SADHANA)

LESSON 10: YOGA OF ACTION

Yoga done in the form of action consists of {2.1}

1. Endurance*
2. Self-study
3. Surrendering to the Supreme

This (yoga of action) is practised for the sake of attaining the attitude required for absorption and reducing pain-causing thought patterns. {2.2}

Klesha (pain-causing thought patterns) can be remembered as a tree. Ignorance is the root of the tree, which enables all other klesha. False identification, attraction, aversion and fear of death, are each one of the main branches of this tree, that can give rise to many other pain causing branches and sub branches.

LESSON 11: SOURCES OF SUFFERING

These pain-causing thought patterns (referred as 'klesha' in Sanskrit) are, {2.3}

1. Ignorance
2. False Identification
3. Attraction
4. Aversion
5. Fear of death (losing identity)

All of these arise from ignorance and their state can vary between {2.4}

1. Dormant
2. Weakened
3. Interrupted or
4. Dominant

Ignorance is the act of mistaking any of the following {2.5}

1. Impermanent to be permanent
2. Impure to be pure
3. Pain to be pleasure
4. Non-self to be self

False identification is confusing one's pure consciousness with one's capability to perceive. {2.6}

Attraction comes as result of pleasure. {2.7}

Aversion comes as result of pain. {2.8}

With a momentum of its own, affecting even the wise, is the fear of death (losing identity). {2.9}

May peace and conflict co-exist

without one sabotaging the other.

For they both have a purpose

and a reason that goes beyond,

what the lay mind can comprehend.

Peace is the end of a cycle

while conflict is the beginning of a new,

an element so crucial

that without it, peace cannot dwell.

LESSON 12: ELIMINATING SUFFERING

All these 'klesha' (5 pain-causing thought patterns mentioned in 2.3) can be nullified by tracing back to their origin, when they are subtle (just arising). {2.10}

When the 'klesha' have grown and are causing fluctuations in the mind, they can be removed through meditation. {2.11}

Arising from these klesha one builds up a repository of consequences (referred as 'karma' in Sanskrit), that are experienced during this lifetime or will be experienced in later lifetimes. {2.12}

Depending on that (karma), one experiences outcomes in the form of class of birth, life span and happiness. {2.13}

The happiness and suffering experienced by one, are outcomes caused by virtuous and non-virtuous activities one has performed. {2.14}

The wise see change, pain, mental impressions, acting in contradiction to one's nature and suffering as being universal. {2.15}

And hence consciously eliminate that which can cause suffering in future (the 5 pain causing thought patterns mentioned in 2.3). {2.16}

Confusing the perceiver and the perceived (item 4 of 2.5) is the root cause (of suffering) and can be removed. {2.17}

Evolution of Consciousness

interpreted from Sankhya Sutra by Kapila using illustrations of Swami J

5 senses of cognition (jnanendriya) are seeing, smelling, hearing, tasting and touching
5 senses of action (karmendriya) are speaking, moving, grasping, reproducing and eliminating
5 subtle elements (tanmatra) are form, odour, sound, flavour and touch
5 gross elements (mahabhuta) are earth, fire, water, air and space

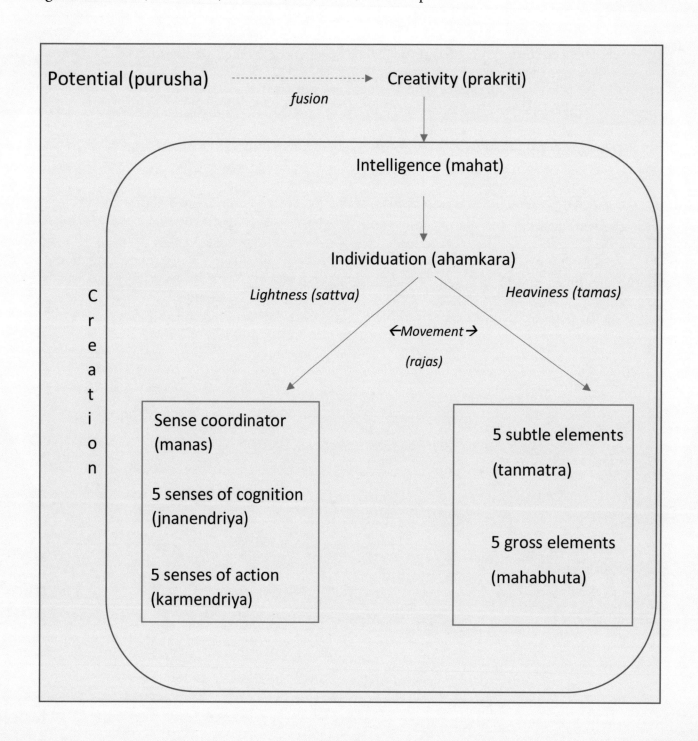

LESSON 13: PERCIEVABLE WORLD

Displaying qualities of lightness (sattva), action (rajas) and firmness (tamas) and made from elements (air, water, fire, earth, space) is the perceivable world, which is made for the purpose of (a) enjoyment and (b) liberation. {2.18}

The (three) qualities vary from specialised, standard, definable and beyond definition. {2.19}

Though coloured by the mind, that which perceives, is pure consciousness. {2.20}

And all of that which is seen exists only for the sake of that which sees (pure consciousness). {2.21}

After achieving its purpose, a certain perception may disappear from the reality of one who has overcome it, but it continues to exist for others. {2.22}

* Seven levels of unfoldment of wisdom as it appeared in my meditation. (Yoga Sutra does not explain what these 7 levels are and hence I meditated on this and following is as it appeared to me.) I encourage you to meditate on this yourself, to find your truth.

1. Truth 2. Love 3. Equality 4. Humbleness 5. Reverence 6. Rest 7. Joy

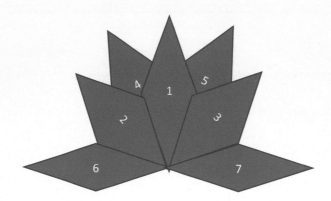

LESSON 14: ACHIEVING LIBERATION

Identifying oneself with one's form (appearance) instead of the potential to be one's own master, is the cause of false union. {2.23}

And this is the cause of ignorance (this and the above sutra reinstates what was mentioned in 2.17). {2.24}

When the false union is overcome, one experiences liberation. {2.25}

Continuous flow of discriminatory wisdom is the means to achieve this goal. {2.26}

This happens through seven* levels of unfoldment of wisdom. {2.27}

<u>Panchakosh (5 sheaths) Theory & 8 Limb Method:</u> Below I have outlined how the 8-limb method recommends various techniques to align each of the 5 layers of Self (explained in Upanishads). Please note that this comparison is not mentioned in the Yoga Sutras. This is a map I have drawn between these two theories and is included here to enhance your understanding.

5 Sheaths	Recommended techniques for alignment
Physical	Yoga poses, Sense Withdrawal
Energy	Energy Expansion
Mental	Yama, Niyama, Concentration
Wisdom	Contemplation
Bliss	Absorption

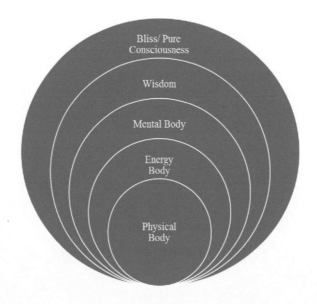

LESSON 15: 8 LIMB METHOD

By practising the limbs of yoga, impurities dissolve, wisdom shines through and continuous flow of discrimination is gained. {2.28}

The eight limbs are, {2.29}

1. Ethical Conduct - Others (Yama)
2. Ethical Conduct - Self (Niyama)
3. Postures (Asana)
4. Energy Expansion/ Breathing techniques (Pranayama)
5. Withdrawal of senses (Pratyahara)
6. Concentration (Dharana)
7. Contemplation (Dhyana)
8. Absorption (Samadhi)

LESSON 16: ETHICAL CONDUCT

Non-violence, truthfulness, non-stealing, practising the presence of divine within and non-greed are the ethical conduct pertaining to others (Yama) {2.30}

Displaying this conduct (Yama) always, regardless of time, place, circumstances and class of birth, is a virtue. {2.31}

Purity (of body and mind), contentment, endurance, self-study and surrender to the supreme, are the ethical conduct pertaining to self (Niyama) {2.32}

*Cultivating the opposite (called *pratipaksha bhavana* in Sanskrit) was practised by ancient yogis to manage negative/ stressful thoughts. Like the new age term, 'positive thinking' pratipaksha bhavana encourages one to focus on the fact that 'the glass is half full'. In simple terms, it is the ability we possess as human beings to look at the other side of the story and search for the silver lining. Being able to catch one-self in the middle of negative thoughts and flipping the coin to focus on something positive/ light/ one can be grateful for, is pratipaksha bhavana. As you can see it is about being mindful of what goes on in your mental space and bringing yourself to a place of positivity, so that you can be in alignment with your true self.

** See below 7 streams of emotions as explained by Swami Jnaneshawara Bharathi. Please note that this has been provided for background information only and is not part of the Yoga Sutras.

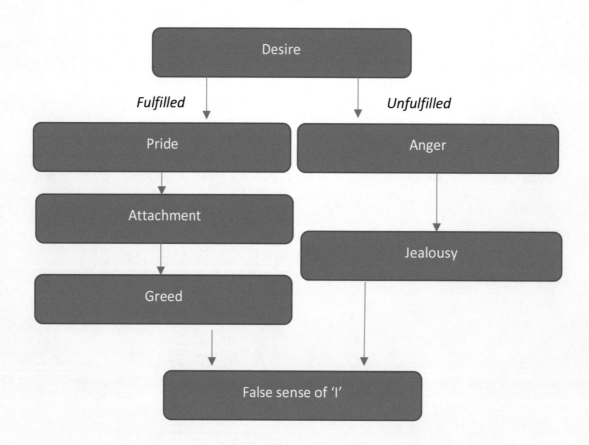

LESSON 17: CULTIVATING THE OPPOSITE

When troublesome thoughts arise, deviating one from the ethical conducts mentioned before, practise cultivating the opposite*. {2.33}

Such (troublesome) thoughts produce unending ignorance and suffering, irrespective of whether

- one is the instigator, the perpetrator or the aggrieved
- the action is provoked by greed, anger or attachment**
- the magnitude is mild, moderate or intense.

Therefore, it is necessary to practise cultivating the opposite. {2.34}

All ethical conducts prescribed (Yama and Niyama) can be understood as a process of cleansing the dirt accumulated on a pond that is unkept. As long as the surface of the pond is covered with dirt it will not be possible to see one's reflection on the pond. Cleaning the dirt on this pond of our mind, accumulated due to attitudes that contradict our true nature is the purpose of Yama and Niyama. Practising these prescribed ethical conducts enables a clear reflection of our true qualities such as those mentioned in lesson 18 and 19.

Sutra 2.40 touches on disinclination from sexual contact and it would be helpful to highlight that while there is nothing wrong with sexual contact, it may be necessary for aspirants to detach from various physical activities to establish a strong connection with one's non-physical self. Various bodily indulgences may require withdrawal, not just sexual contact but also eating, drinking, speaking etc. The purpose of this withdrawal is to be able to learn how to indulge the senses without attachment. As the Zen saying goes, *'Before enlightenment, chop wood, carry water. After enlightenment, chop wood, carry water'*. Thus, it is not about what you do but about how you can do it with non-attachment.

LESSON 18: BENEFITS OF YAMA

When one becomes firmly grounded in non-violence, in their presence others tend to lose any animosity. {2.35}

When one become firmly grounded in truthfulness, results of all actions fall according to their will. {2.36}

When one become firmly grounded in non-stealing, all the riches come towards them. {2.37}

When one becomes firmly grounded in practicing the presence of divine within, their vigour strengthens. {2.38}

When one becomes firmly grounded in non-greed complete knowing occurs regarding the purpose of their birth. {2.39}

LESSON 19: BENEFITS OF NIYAMA

Purity (of body and mind) results in disinclination towards sexual contact. {2.40}

Also comes purity of subtle mental essence, pleasantness, one pointed concentration, control of senses, and capability for self-realisation. {2.41}

Contentment results in supreme level of happiness. {2.42}

Endurance results in all mental impurities being removed and one attains mastery over their body and senses. {2.43}

Self-study results in contact with one's preferred deity. {2.44}

'Surrendering to the supreme' results in increased capability for absorption (samadhi). {2.45}

Components of mind

(adopted from illustrations of Swami Rama)

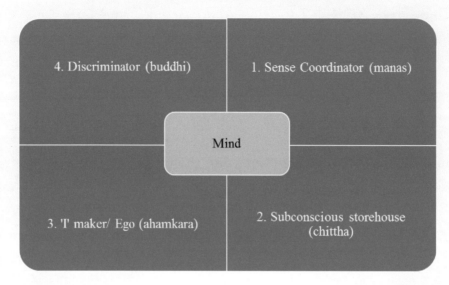

While mind is a common term used to denote various functions, it has 4 main components. The sense co-ordinator (component 1) is responsible for picking up any senses (mentioned in lesson 22) and sending a signal to the brain which then evokes an action. This action taken depends on the content of subconscious storehouse of memories (component 2) and the ego i.e. belief one has about themselves (component 3). For example, if one's senses pick up a sight of a stray dog, they could either run away if they had unpleasant experiences with stray dogs or ignore it, if they do not see themselves as an 'animal person', or make an effort to reach out for the dog and find it's owner, if they believe themselves to someone who cares for animals. These differences in action depends on their memories and beliefs about themselves.

However, apart from these 3 components discussed above, there is a component called 'buddhi' (component 4) which is the discriminator or intellect that has the capacity to make a rational decision based on what is the 'right thing to do' in any given situation. Regardless of whether I see myself as an animal person, I can choose to act responsibly and find the dog's owner. Unless one's buddhi is in charge, a person will continue living a life that resembles their past and feel incapable of making changes in their life.

LESSON 20: YOGIC POSTURES

That which brings stability and ease to one's body is yogic posture. {2.46}

When practised by relaxing physical effort, these postures allow the mind to merge with infinite. {2.47}

Thereafter polarities (dualities) cease to grip the mind. {2.48}

LESSON 21: ENERGY EXPANSION

After accomplishing the postures, one can free/expand their energy by softening their inhale and exhale. {2.49}

Observing the location, duration and number of inhale, exhale and withholding of breath, leads to prolonged and subtle breathing. {2.50}

The fourth level is to transcend the inhale and exhale. {2.51}

Through that the veil concealing the inner light is cast away. {2.52}

This (practise of energy expansion) enables the mind to be suitable and ready for concentration. {2.53}

LESSON 22: WITHDRAWAL OF SENSES

One's senses* have been successfully withdrawn when the mind field (referred as *chittha* in Sanskrit) stands unfused with its activities and resembles its true nature. {2.54}

Then the highest level of mastery/control has been achieved over one's senses. {2.55}

*For more information on 'senses', see explanations for Lesson 13.

Spiritual unfoldment is the process of opening your inner gifts that have been with you all your life.

CHAPTER 3: POWERS (VIBHUTI)

LESSON 23: STEPS TO ABSORPTION

Focussing the attention to one place is called concentration (referred as dharana in Sanskrit). {3.1}

When one's attention flows continuously (uninterrupted by thoughts) towards the object of concentration, it is called contemplation (referred as dhyana in Sanskrit). {3.2}

Absorption (referred as samadhi in Sanskrit) is when the truth (relating to the object of contemplation) alone shines forth transcending its form. {3.3}

When all three techniques mentioned above are practised together it is called samyama. {3.4}

That (samyama) when practised effectively enables access to divine knowledge/ higher consciousness. {3.5}

It (access to divine knowledge) is achieved by practicing the steps mentioned (8 limbs). {3.6}

The last three limbs (of the 8 limbs) are more internal/subtler than the other limbs. {3.7}

However, these (last three limbs) are still external compared to unseeded absorption (mentioned in sutra 1.50). {3.8}

Imagine a still pond at night time. Let's say it is a full moon day and the moon's image is being reflected on the pond. If the moon wants to know itself, it can look at the reflection and say to itself, 'I am that'. Now if you pick up some pebbles and throw it into the pond, you will create ripples that will distort the image of the moon being reflected. If you throw pebbles continuously, the reflection will become so distorted that it may look nothing like the moon.

This moon is a metaphorical simile that represents every human being on the quest to know themselves. The pond is a simile that represents the mind field of that human being. So, for a human being to fully know themselves, there are 3 pre-requisites.

1. The pond needs be stilled i.e. mental fluctuations (throwing of pebbles in the above metaphor) need to be mastered. This requisite is called 'nirodah' and is referred in sutra 3.9
2. The ability to get fully absorbed in that which is the point of focus (reflection of the moon in above metaphor) to connect with its true nature, transcending its form, needs to be mastered. This requisite is called 'samadhi' and is referred in sutra 3.11
3. The ability to continuously focus on the same subject (the reflection of the moon on the pond) for long period of time, needs to be established. This requisite is called 'ekagrata' and is referred in sutra 3.12

These 3 pre-requisites, in my opinion, can be achieved from bottom up i.e., 1. ekagrata, 2. samadhi and then 3. nirodah. After these 3 have been achieved one can know themselves by understanding the nature (the growing and the fading over a 28 day and night cycle, in the example of a moon), characteristics (the moon having craters for example) and the state (which phase the moon is currently at i.e. growing or fading and at what level).

LESSON 24: EVOLUTION

Evolution towards mastery (over tendencies of the mind) occurs when the impressions made by moments of mastery, exceed other existing impressions {3.9}

This evolution is completed by repeated practise thereby creating deep impression on the mind. {3.10}

As one's tendency to be scattered declines and the tendency to be one-pointed strengthens, evolution towards samadhi occurs. {3.11}

Evolution towards one-pointedness occurs when arising and subsiding thoughts/ cognitions are of similar nature. {3.12}

In this state of being, the nature, characteristics and state of one's makeup can be understood. {3.13}

Past, present and future follows the trajectory of one's nature. {3.14}

The changes in one's apparent state is due to the difference in states along that trajectory. {3.15}

By practising all three evolutionary states described (in 3.9, 3.11 and 3.12) at the same time, one can gain knowledge of their past and future. {3.16}

Following this sutra, Patanjali explains various powers (levitation, invisibility, shape-shifting, contact with non-physical beings, extra sensory sight, hearing, mind reading, remote vision, controlling hunger and thirst etc) that one can attain through the practice of samyama. However, in between those explanations Patanjali also mentions that these abilities may seem like advancements to a materialistic mind, however they are obstacles to enlightenment and therefore one should set them aside with detachment. To stay true to the purpose of this book, I refrain from delving into those sutras. It would be enough to comment that if you experience anything seemingly super-human, in your journey to enlightenment or after, bear in mind Patanjali's suggestion and practise detachment.

To enable your understanding of Yoga Sutra references to 'seeing the sequence simultaneously' in sutra 3.52 and later in sutra 4.22, the following extract from the book, Home with God by Neale Donald Walsch, has been included.

Let's say you have walked into a room. It is a huge room and an ornate one. Perhaps it is a library in a richly appointed home. You walk into the room and notice some things first. May be some larger than life statues, a stuffed bear or blaring TV. Your attention goes there at once. Now you begin to look around and you start to see other things, smaller things, less dramatic things. Finally, you move towards a bookcase in the middle of the room. Your eyes light upon a title. This is what you came into this room for. Describing this scene to someone later you might say "at last there it was!" but there is no at last about it. You could just as easily have said, "at first, there it was!" everything in that room existed simultaneously but you experienced it sequentially. Thus, the moment was truly 'sequentaneous'.

In Ultimate Reality, things ARE there before you see them. That is, multiple possibilities exist at all times. Every conceivable outcome of every conceivable situation exists right here, right now – and is occurring right here right now.

Applying the above extract to the topic of discrimination (lesson 25) and perceiving the perceiver (lesson 30), we could say that to understand how the mind works, it is essential to realise that the beginning, the middle and end of our thought sequences exist simultaneously at all times, although we may experience it as a sequence.

LESSON 25: DISCRIMINATION

Learning to distinguish between the purest aspect of one's mind and one's pure consciousness (purusha) brings omnipotence and omniscience. {3.49}

Non-attachment to that too results in destruction of seeds of bondage and thus liberation is achieved. {3.50}

There is no need to be proud of offers of high spiritual positions as doing so will result in relapse of bondage. {3.51}

Through samyama on moments and their succession, one achieves discriminative insight. {3.52}

Thus, one is able to distinguish between aspects that may appear similar in category, characteristics or location. {3.53}

Discriminative insight is ability to comprehend sequential aspects simultaneously. {3.54}

When the purest aspect of one's mind attains the same level of purity as one' pure consciousness, one attains liberation. {3.55}

From nothing comes everything.
Into nothing goes everything.

CHAPTER 4: LIBERATION (KAIVALYA)

LESSON 26: TRANSFORMATION

Attainment of powers (mentioned in chapter 3) can come by birth, using herbs, chanting mantras or through samadhi. {4.1}

Inner transformation carries through to the external. {4.2}

External transformation is ineffective and all one needs to do is re-form the pathways like a farmer. {4.3}

LESSON 27: ACHIEVING MENTAL STILLNESS

The mind is created by 'I' sense. {4.4}

To break through mental fluctuations (mentioned in 1.6) it is essential to realise that the singular mind is the instigator of all mental fluctuations. {4.5}

The mind that is born out of meditation is free of fluctuation. {4.6}

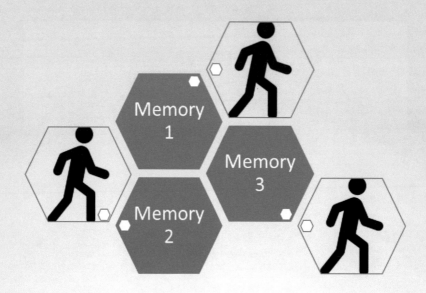

The cause and effect relationship between memory and karmic impression can be understood better with an example. Say that a child was abandoned by it's care giver at a very young age, for example their care giver died. This child has a subconscious memory of being abandoned. This is the first impression which will then keep gathering magnitude as the child experiences anything remotely similar to abandonment e.g. a friend in the child's primary school moves town, a teacher the child is attached to dies etc. Now the impression of abandonment is strongly laid in the child's mind and will continue to gather momentum until the effect created by the memory is retained. The cause here being the memory and 'feeling of abandonment' being the effect. In therapeutic setting I use Time Based Therapy (TBT) which enables a person through hypnosis, to access the earliest memory that created the emotion and disconnect the memory from the emotion. TBT works very effectively in disconnecting the cause and effect thereby setting the person free to experience life differently. I encourage you to explore modalities such as TBT, if you have strong patterns you notice in your life.

LESSON 28: CAUSE & EFFECT

Consequences of action (karma) are neither white nor black for a yogi while they are threefold for others. {4.7}

These (threefold karma) later ripen and manifest accordingly. {4.8}

Category, time and place of these (karmic) manifestations can seem interrupted (see sutra 2.4) even though they are continuous, due to memory and impressions caused by memories, appearing as one. {4.9}

There is no beginning to these (karmic impressions) as the desire to live, is eternal. {4.10}

As these (karmic impressions) are held in place due to the cause and effect principle, they (karmic impressions) disappear when the later (effect) disappears. {4.11}

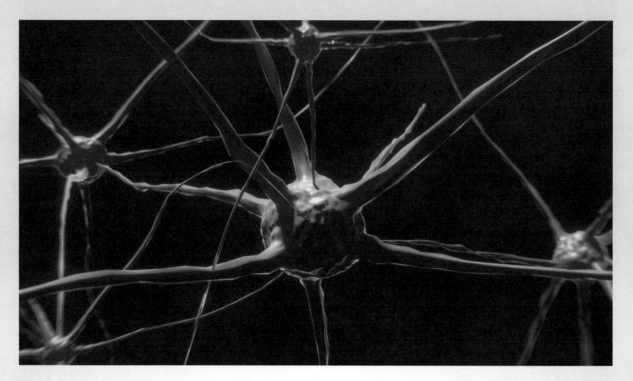

Yoga Sutra references to 'pathways' can be understood as the neural pathways in one's brain. As research supporting neuro science indicates, all human behaviours are the result of pathways established in one's brain. The reverse is also true - through adopting new behaviours, human beings can establish new neural pathways or extinguish pathways by discontinuing old habits. In this light, sutras 4.3 and 4.12 to 4.15 can be understood. For further understanding of changing your neural pathways I highly recommend learning NLP (Neuro Linguistic Programming) which is an applied science that I have used on myself and various others seeking to recreate their life anew.

LESSON 29: METHOD OF THE MIND

Past and future are bound by the pathways in one's mind. {4.12}

These can be apparent or subtle and are made of three basic qualities (guna). {4.13}

All transformations are based on the same principle. {4.14}

While objects are the same, perception varies due to the difference in pathways. {4.15}

However, no single perception governs the object for if it did, what would happen if the object wasn't perceived. {4.16}

Objects are perceived wisely or otherwise based on the colouring of one's mind and its expectations. {4.17}

LESSON 30: PERCEIVING THE PERCEIVER

All fluctuations of the mind are known by its master, the changeless pure consciousness. {4.18}

But the mind isn't self-illuminating while it is engaged in perception. {4.19}

Nor can both be cognised simultaneously. {4.20}

When attempted one might get overloaded with memories and impressions. {4.21}

When one can see the sequence simultaneously, knowledge of how the mind works can be attained. {4.22}

When the seer cognises, the seen and the colouring (that causes them to see it in a particular way), everything is understood. {4.23}

Countless impressions from the past and different ways of perception exist only due to their co-morbidity. {4.24}

Once the unique perception of the soul has been witnessed, all mental fluctuations cease. {4.25}

*The highest form of freedom
is freedom from your own thoughts.*

LESSON 31: COMPLETE LIBERATION

That discernment enables the mind to flow towards liberation, like (a stone) rolling from high point to low point of a mountain. {4.26}

This (process of liberation) can be interrupted by arising impressions from the past. {4.27}

Those interruptions can be removed by following the same process described for removing klesha (see Lesson 12) {4.28}

When there is an attitude of dispassion towards everything including the infinite, wisdom pours on one like rain. {4.29}

Then one experiences complete cessation of pain causing thoughts (klesha) and consequences (karma). {4.30}

With all veils and impurities removed, one comes in contact with infinite wisdom and there is hardly anything left to be known. {4.31}

Having accomplished their purpose, the three basic qualities (guna) cease to influence one's thought sequence. {4.32}

With pure consciousness having no more motive, the three qualities having receded to its pre-birth state, liberation achieved, one's identity rests on their true nature and such is the power of mind.

This concludes the Yoga Sutra text

APPENDIX: A

Testimonials

Some testimonials from people learning the Yoga Sutras, follow. These people are from various walks of life and meet weekly at Hridhaya Centre for Wellbeing in Mackay, Queensland, to share their learning.

The purpose of including the following testimonials, is to bring hope and encouragement to those who may be just starting or feeling overwhelmed by the arduous task of recreating their life. May the words of these everyday souls, inspire you to venture on.

"On my run to escape materialism, the statement of practising non-attachment crossed my path, during Yoga Sutra study. Not to be attached, to not only objects but also people, roles, habits, situations, memories, approval and judgements is, to me, the true embodiment of freedom."

- Petra

"*I am more aware of my attachment to objects and the people closest to me. I can let go and trust that things will work out. I am not my thoughts, I am not my actions, I am Soul.*"

- Joan

"*I find OM chants harmonising, reverberating through my body. I find it a perfect step to meditation. It helps in calming the mind and make meditation easier to approach.*"

- Tony

"The biggest growth I have experienced through Yoga Sutra study is learning to be aware and being responsible for my part in relationship with others. I am mindful how I react in any situation now, knowing that I am a reflection of that person!"

- Karen

"I find the consistency to practise, for I am worthy of this time alone with me. With the study group, I find new friends and I come to learn that I am my own best friend, someone who has been hidden for far too long. I grow stronger with this knowledge. In this space, I am aligned with my spiritual belief that we are all of one source. I have found my place of healing, love and light."

- *Kay*

"Yoga Sutra study has been like putting a jigsaw puzzle together, providing an explanation for a lot of personal growth I have gone through over the years, in my awakening. I find it easier now, to let go and have trust in the universe, that I am where I am supposed to be, at this time. This has brought greater awareness making me more conscious in creating inner peace at a deeper level."

- Donna

"*I find peace in these lessons. I love 'OM'ing. It is simple, and I like it. I have also come to accept that you are never just something, be it a mother, a daughter or whatever you are telling yourself.*"

- Robyn

"I have found a new understanding of myself, about disease and about meditation. The lessons offer me clarity to find my purpose and trust that the universe will show me the path, if I still my mind and listen."

- Melinda

"My relationship with my son has changed. He is diagnosed with ADHD and Aspergers. He also has some mental health challenges. I used to see him as someone I had to fix. Now I am focussing more on his positive attributes and the things he is good at. He is such a beautiful charismatic boy, a great conversationalist and very intelligent. This has not only been beneficial for me but for him too. I see him standing taller now and accepting himself more."

- Miranda

"What I like and what I am uncomfortable with in another person, is also within me. I know to go there now. I feel I've just begun again, realising and understanding I have the power and choice to break my patterns, stop giving my power away, step back, then respond for my highest good."

- Robyn

"What I found helpful was learning to be comfortable with my own self and not be controlled by objects, for example, new big house, new latest iPhone. I don't need these objects to make me feel happy. To me, being asleep is being gripped by the 'must have's and being awake is spending time with loved ones and experiencing life."

- Sandy

"I understand what the word 'ego' means. I can see how life and my memories have shaped me and given me several attributes, I believe about myself. For example, I am tardy, I like to make my bed before leaving home, I am healthy person, I like everything to match, I am not a story teller, I am no good at writing and so on. All these I statements can be me if I want them to be, but they don't have to be me. I am so much more and can be whatever I want to be. I statements are not permanent. They are fluid and changeable."

"I have been able to raise and maintain my vibration. Detachment from physical and material things has become easier. My understanding of myself, the universe and where I am in the grand scheme of things has become deeper, thanks to Yoga Sutras"

"I have found the importance of self-dialogue, self-belief and self-worth - to know the keys and triggers to let go of, to be calm, not to react, knowledge that we alone are responsible for our own actions and to take an alternate approach, rather than negative response."

"Understanding the concept of withdrawal from senses was very powerful for me. Just that morning before we discussed this lesson, I had heard a song on the radio that took me right back to when I was younger and had my heart broken. It brought up lots of sadness and put me in a strange state. I certainly wasn't in the present! Then after studying this lesson on sense withdrawal, I understood that hearing the song prompted my subconscious storehouse to bring up a memory and once I was in that state it was very hard to come back. Next time I heard that song, I was more aware of the process and told myself just to enjoy the song and that I don't need to go 'there'!

"Meditation offers me serenity in a confusing world. I become aware of my own internal domestic violence. I realise that no one can make me feel any specific way and that I can be my own worst enemy. I come to see that we can't pour from an empty cup."

"I have learnt that I don't have to fix everything and everyone. I can just observe and examine my own responses, reactions and what that tells me about myself."

"Perhaps the greatest gem of all learnings was to finally understand what it means to surrender. The perfect example was when I was trying to become debt free. Nothing was happening, and my credit card bills were mounting up. After discussion, I realised that my focus was still on debt and made me wonder what it would be

like to be debt free. Financial freedom came to me as words that reflected what I was wanting. Through Yoga Sutra study, I learnt that to achieve something you also need to surrender. To do that I had to realise that my pure consciousness was OK no matter whether I had debts up to my eyeballs or no debt. I had to fully accept and embody that. Once I did, our financial status began to shift almost immediately. We finally sold our truck and paid off the credit cards! Suddenly my dream of financial freedom had become much more attainable."

"What these lessons have taught me is to let go of expectations and just be. Finding myself inside the stillness, finding the divine within and finding that I am the driver of my life, I now accept what is and find my authentic self."

APPENDIX: B

What is Enlightenment?

Spiritual enlightenment is neither understood nor seen as an approachable goal, by many. While some have been led to believe that it is a special status reserved for a chosen few people only, there are others who mistake super normal powers (described in chapter 3 of Yoga Sutras) to be enlightenment. However, enlightenment is a natural human need that arises after the fulfillment of other basic needs (described by psychologist, Abraham Maslow) such as biological satisfaction, safety, food, shelter, love, belonging, self-esteem and intellectual fulfillment.

Just as human being becomes curious about their physical health and mental health, spiritual health also becomes a topic of interest when the individual's surrounding enables it. Hence it is necessary for us, as a human race to understand and break the taboo around enlightenment. While the term itself means 'to arrive at an understanding of something', spiritual enlightenment is simply knowing our spiritual self. Yoga Sutras help us do this by encouraging a direct experience of one's spiritual self and provides us with a systematic process and definitions of various stages in the process.

Until one reaches a sense of complete acceptance and appreciation for human life, the knowledge of 'who we are' spiritually is insufficient, maladaptive and is only half the journey towards enlightenment. To further explain this, I would like to share a story from Mahabharata, an epic from India.

Abhimanyu was the son of Arjuna, a skilled warrior of Pandava clan and nephew of Krishna, a human incarnation of Lord Vishnu. When Abhimanyu was in his mother Subhadra's womb, Krishna indulged her with stories of his victories. One day Krishna was telling Subhadra how he broke the plot of 'chakravyuha' - an arrangement in the battlefield were soldiers form a maze making it difficult for the enemy troop to enter and defeat them. As Krishna completed narrating how he entered the formation and was about to start explaining how to exit, he realised that Subhadra was asleep and the acknowledgment voice he was hearing was from the child in her womb, Abhimanyu. Taken back, Krishna stopped his narration thinking to himself, "This child is so eager even before it is born. If I narrate how to exit the formation, he will be invincible in wars and I will need to reincarnate to come back and conquer him". Thus, Abhimanyu was born with the knowledge of breaking through the 'chakravyuha' formation and did so during the Mahabharata war. However, since he didn't know how to exit, he got killed in the battle.

This story, I feel, is a great simile to explain the process of enlightenment. Like Abhimanyu most of us who are intrigued by the concept of 'knowing oneself' seem to intuitively figure our way through. We may have experiences that are out of ordinary and struggle to explain it or be understood by others around. We may feel like a misfit and question our journey. We may find ourselves frustrated with not knowing how to re-integrate with the world around. The physical world can seem like a daunting place filled with misery and ignorance, and re-integrating with physical life, which we may have once enjoyed, can be challenging. This is where, the real work begins.

While self-realisation is intuitive, re-integration, is in most cases new the soul and can be achieved only through commitment and faith that 'all is well and perfect in every way' even when one's daily experience does not feel so. Continuing with one's practise of meditation and various other methods described in the Yoga Sutras, one can gradually start to re-integrate and begin living a normal life, with an extra normal awareness of self. As Sankhya Sutras state, one becomes 'a rope amongst snakes', looking more or less the same as others, but completely reformed, inside out. Reaching a level of knowing and acceptance, where one can involve themselves in daily life, appreciating and enjoying the pleasures of physical life without getting fused with them, retaining full awareness of the self, is the final stage of 'enlightenment'.

APPENDIX: C

Where is the end?

While it is tempting to think that one can go through various steps (including those recommended by Yoga Sutras) and reach a point where there is nothing more to be done, life isn't so. Fortunately, there is always some aspect of our life where we may need to apply our knowing, come back to the place of complete awareness and live as an embodiment of 'who we are'. This journey of enlightenment is a daily process and there is no end to it.

However, once a person begins to experience the levels of 'absorption' described in Yoga Sutras, major shifts become evident. Firstly, faith in life and its perfection strengthens. Their ego centre shifts to become more inclusive of others. As a result, self-worth, confidence and belief in oneself increases. Life becomes much easier to manage and more within one's control than not. The person becomes more adept to recognising and eliminating stress causing patterns. They tend to catch themselves when they are out of alignment and bring themselves back into alignment frequently and hence experiences synchronicity in manifesting their desires. They are also more likely to not sway too far from their purpose, due the increased level of self-awareness. Freewill and power of choice becomes a living truth. For such a person, the search for self, god and the quest to understand the meaning of life often ends, but the journey of living life as an expression of one's true self continues. In other words, the moon's quest to know itself ends however, fulfilling the duty of shining it's light each night continues on…

About Prabha:

Prabha Srinivasan is Counsellor, Life Coach and Yoga teacher. Prabha was brought up in southern India deeply immersed in the cultural and religious practices of the time. Growing up, Prabha felt a pull to go beyond the current practices and be guided by her heart. As part of this growing up process, Prabha encountered various challenging life situations that moulded her and deepened the need to understand life. All of Prabha's work today have been inspired by the hardships she faced and the will to 'crack to the code' of life.

Prabha founded Hridhaya Centre for Wellbeing, in 2016, to promote spiritual growth and to foster the community during their soul's emergence. Hridhaya has now grown to become a hub for wellbeing.

Prabha lives in Mackay, Queensland and endeavours to continue learning and sharing life with all. More about Prabha's work can be found at www.shftinside.com or www.hridhaya.org

Prabha is also the author of the book, Guidance In Your Handbag, a collection of 100 thoughts for everyday inspiration.

Printed in the United States
By Bookmasters